I0467968

Start Your Dream Business Today!

Must-Know Strategies to Launch a Successful Business (And Tips To Keep It Running!)

Revised Second Edition

Biba Pédron

ISBN: 1500504386
ISBN-13: 978-1500504380

With love to the wind beneath my wings, my parents, Liliane and Michel, who always support me.

CONTENTS

CONTENTS

FOREWORD

When I met Ms. Biba Pédron at the turn of the 21st Century she had just built her first successful communication business in France. Through our trusted business association I have always been impressed with Biba's concern to help people succeed and her power networking skills as she deftly connects people for mutually beneficial relationships. Through real life stories told from her heart, Biba shares her experiences in this book to save you time, money and increase your chances of succeeding with starting a business.

Whether you do it part time to supplement a job income or you make it a full time commitment, there is no better time to start a business than right now. When starting a business, I advise my coaching clients to take advice ONLY from people who have accomplished what you want to achieve. Overcoming many challenges Biba Pédron shares true to life business success in her book "Start Your Dream Business Today". Providing step by step procedures in each chapter, Biba eliminates the guess work and fear of being a business owner.

From writing a business plan to networking and acquiring clients, reading "Start Your Dream Business Today" is your entrepreneur road map for success. I know many successful business owners have achieved success from Biba Pédron's coaching services. Think of this book as Biba being your personal coach you can reference everyday as you develop your business to achieve your financial goals and create a better life style for your family.

I wish you well on your journey to business owner success. I am confident "Start Your Dream Business Today" can help you get there.

Carl E. REID, CSI
Successful Entrepreneur and Intrapreneur
Author of "10 Powerful Networking Secrets Of Influential People"
& "10 Powerful Networking Tips Using Business Cards Extended Global Edition"
www.CarlEReid.com

How I Realized
My American Dream

In order to understand why I decided to write this book, I would like to tell you a little about my story and how I started successful businesses both in France and in the United States.

In 1992, I came to the United States for the first time to spend a month's vacation. I traveled from New York to San Francisco in a minivan with 12 other people. It was my best vacation ever.

As soon as I landed at JFK Airport in New York and discovered Manhattan, I immediately felt right at home. People often ask me why I like New York so much, but I can't explain it. It is like it was my destiny. Or maybe I lived here in a past life, who knows? It was a longstanding dream of mine to come to the US, and I was finally here!

At first, I didn't really plan to live here, but after that wonderful month, I knew that I would move to the United States one day. I didn't know when; I didn't know how; and I didn't know what I would do. I just knew I would live here one day and start a fantastic venture. At that time, I was working for the sales department of one of the biggest office supplies companies in France, making lots of money with a very easy job. You can't imagine how much money you can make, just selling pens, pencils, paper, ink or other stuff like that. I had a very conformable life, a lot of money, and lots of vacation time. Nothing to complain about. I just didn't have any passion for what I was doing.

I came back to the US, mainly to New York, many times over the next few years to vacation and to improve my English, but also to learn more about this country which fascinated me so much. When I left New York at the end of the summer of 1997, I made a decision to start a business in France; my main goal was to be free to travel the way I wanted, so I would not have to wait for my next vacation.

As soon as I came back to Paris, I did some research to see what kind of businesses I could start on my own.

I had been a sales and marketing manager for almost 15 years, so if I was able to manage other people's companies, I thought that I could do the same for my own business. Plus, I was a bit bored and liked the prospect of putting wealth into my pocket instead of my employer. I wanted to start a business I could run from anywhere in the world with only a phone, a computer and Internet access. I conducted a lot of research and spent months reading books, articles and reports before deciding what to do.

At the beginning of 1998, I had just turned 35 years old, and was ready for a new exciting challenge. I launched F.P Communication, a telemarketing company. I quit my job one Friday evening and started my business on Monday morning, without any clients or any great amount of savings. When I think back, it was really crazy and, in a way, really irresponsible.

But I was so determined I knew it would work. I started looking for clients and was lucky enough to find my first one the very first week, so I was highly encouraged.

I advertised, sent direct mail pieces, launched e-mail campaigns and very quickly attracted a few clients—small business owners who didn't have the money to maintain their own sales teams, but who definitely needed to promote their businesses, so that they could make more money.

With my background, experience, and skills as a marketing manager, I was able to help them develop their marketing and sales departments, organize direct mail campaigns, make cold calls to develop their client databases, set up appointments and negotiate contracts.

For the first twelve months, I worked seven days a week, 14 to 16 hours a day. This commitment was essential to getting my business off the ground. Then the venture became so successful that I didn't even have to advertise or promote it anymore. I had all my clients, and more than I could handle, just by word of mouth.

For two years, I didn't come back to New York. I was so busy running my business I didn't have time for anything else. Afterward, I decided it was time to hire a team so I would have more time to do what I wanted and work "on my business" and not "in my business" as Michael Gerber explains in his book "The E-Myth Revisited". After all, I started this business to have more freedom, not to become an employee or perhaps the sole employee of my own business.

I came to New York for two weeks to see if, as I had hoped, I could run my business from anywhere. Of course, I informed my clients just in case any technical problems with the Internet arose, and I wanted to make sure that I could continue my cold-calling efforts without difficulties.

Not only did the companies I cold-called not notice I was calling them from the US, but when I came back to Paris and contacted my own clients to let them know I was back, before I got the chance to say anything, most of them asked, "When are you supposed to leave for New York?"

They didn't realize I had left and already returned... especially since everything was done the same way with the same high level of quality and they continued to receive their weekly reports on time. They didn't notice any difference!

That day, I knew I succeeded.

Now I could travel as frequently as I wanted, without worrying whether I would lose my clients. Everything was working perfectly.

A few months later, I came back to New York to see if I could expand my company and locate US small business owners who wanted to develop their businesses in France. I believed I could help them set up appointments, make cold calls and organize their trips to France.

Almost by accident, I discovered the world of networking.

Networking didn't exist in my world in France at that time so the concept of networking was completely new to me.

I still remember the very first networking event I attended in New York. I discovered the event on the Internet and signed-up. I arrived in a crowded bar, very noisy, took my name-tag, and looked around. I was so intimidated I left in less than two minutes and said "Ok, this networking thing is definitely not for me."

Looking back, this is quite funny when you consider that I later started my own business to organize and facilitate networking events!

I wouldn't accept failure, so several weeks later, I decided to attend another event, only to discover the same thing—a crowded bar, very noisy, and extremely difficult to meet people and conduct business. Again, I took my name-tag, except I decided I would not leave before I spoke with at least two people.

Actually though, I cheated. I stayed in a corner clutching my glass and waited for someone to come over to speak with me.

But that night was my first victory. Afterward I attended more and more events. I set goals to speak with four people, then six people, then ten, etc. But I quickly realized I wouldn't find clients for my current telemarketing company because small businesses had more than enough opportunities in the United States and didn't really need to expand their businesses in France. I was quite disappointed because I had spent the last two years building a business I couldn't expand to the US. What was I going to do?

I didn't really like attending the networking events in crowded, noisy bars. At that time, I was not completely fluent in English, and it was often difficult to understand what people were saying to me, especially with the noise. Plus, I was really not comfortable in the middle of these crowds and wasn't able to use them to grow my business.

That was when I decided to start my own networking events, smaller and more intimate events, where people would be able to have conversations and not have to shout at each other. They would have time to introduce themselves and their businesses and not merely exchange their business cards in three seconds before thrusting their card at the next person.

So here again, a few years after I started my first business in Paris, I was ready to start my second one, from scratch, in New York City. But this time I knew it would be more difficult because this was not my home country and English was not my first language.

I needed to get a visa and I knew I wouldn't be able to start my second business literally overnight as I had started the first time. It took two more years before I was able to incorporate as a business and get started. During that time, I traveled to New York often to work on my new business venture. My personal experiences and desire to start a business in the United States made it possible for me to learn a lot about how to start a business.

I attended every business seminar I could find and I spent every afternoon of the summer of 2001 at the New York Public Library. I read every book I could find about starting a business, how and where to incorporate, how to write a business plan, how to write a proposal, how to develop strategies, how to develop a marketing plan, and especially, learning how to do business the "American way." I spent hours and hours studying all of these subjects.

When I was finally ready to start my new venture, I contacted various lawyers to see how to start the process to obtain my visa. I met with a number of attorneys who essentially discouraged me from starting a new business. The common theme was "You don't have enough money," or "You don't have enough experience to start a business here."

Some "advisors" told me I needed one million dollars to start a business; others said I needed to invest at least a hundred thousand dollars to get the visa. I spent months and months, traveling between Paris and New York, and spoke to numerous lawyers but always got the same answers.

One of my strengths is that I never take "NO" for an answer. I couldn't be the first person to move from France to the US to start a business! So I continued my research until I finally found the lawyer who was able to give me the right information to start my business. After that, it took another four months to write, rewrite, and revise my business plan, another month to incorporate, and a couple of more months to send my application to the American Embassy in Paris before I finally received my visa.

So as you see, I spent a lot of time studying this topic: "How to Start Your Own Business." And from personal experience, I know how difficult it is to walk through this entire process. That's why I now dedicate part of my time to helping people realize their own American Dream.

When I came back to New York with my visa in my pocket, I was extremely happy because I was realizing my dream. I was able to start a business in America. My goal was to run and grow a company designed to organize networking events, which would help people grow their businesses, meet other people, build their circle of contacts.

But soon, many people, both French and American, asked me for advice and help on starting their own businesses. People were asking me more and more how I grew my business so quickly starting 2 years before without speaking English and no contacts. At first, I helped them one at a time, for free giving them advice on how to structure their business and more. Then one of my business mentors suggested since I was already organizing networking meetings, I should organize seminars and coach people to start and grow their business.

That is how I became a business coach, that I really enjoy doing until today, helping thousands of people grow their businesses, attract more clients and make more money.

Then one day I went to Miami to visit a friend for three days. I had never visited Miami before (or Florida) and fell in love with the weather. The winters in New York were getting colder and colder and I just couldn't stand it anymore, even though I LOVE New York. So I made the decision right there it was time to move. And the best part is, like the decision I made in 1998 when I started my first business that I could operate from anywhere in the world with a phone, a computer and an Internet connection, I was able to move my business to Florida and continue to coach my clients without losing any money or risking my business.

For the past 2 years, I also coached entrepreneurs in France and was lucky to be recognized as one of the top business coaches, bringing my American experience and strategies to the French word.

I am very lucky to have a business I love that I designed for myself and having great clients and raving fans while I have the perfect lifestyle. I was able to achieve my American Dream.

Since you're reading this book, it means I have succeeded in my goal in helping thousands of people. I would be delighted if my experiences can help you either make the decision to start your own business or if I can save you time and money in the process and help you build wealth faster. And more importantly: to help you live YOUR dream.

PART I
How to Get Started

CHAPTER 1
Stop Looking for a Job &
Start Your Own Business!

I had worked for sales and marketing departments in various companies for 15 years and realized that my passion was to create, to build, and to control. While I may have been a bit impulsive when I quit my job that Friday night in 1998, I have never regretted that decision for one second. I realized I would never be satisfied until I gave it a shot and tried to start my own business.

While the following questions only offer a glimpse into the reasons why you may decide to start your own business, take some time to answer these questions:

1. Do you enjoy your job?
2. Would you rather be doing something else than going to work every day?
3. Do you feel that your current career path provides enough fulfillment and advancement possibilities?
4. Do you believe you could do better in your own company?
5. If you work for someone else's company, are you concerned about the long-term viability of your position? Your career path? What is the likelihood you could get laid off? If you get laid off, how long will it take you to find a new position?
6. Are employee benefits a large portion of your compensation

package? Could you afford to pay these costs out of your own pocket?

7. If you found something exciting to do on your own, would you be willing to work 12 to 14 hours every day?

8. Are you a self-starter? In other words, are you the kind of person who can make a plan, prioritize the steps, manage your time, and implement your plan?

If you answered YES to these 8 questions, stop wasting your time, start your own business!

Let's say your supervisor gave you a great performance review in your last position, maybe you developed a new program that grew the department's performance by 20%, or you were the best salesperson in your department for a few months. You have all the skills required to be a great manager, or a great salesperson, and you know the competition and you know your market. So maybe you already have what it takes to be a successful entrepreneur.

So then ask yourself this question: What's holding you back? Are you making excuses for why you're staying in your present position rather than embarking on your own business?

When you are on your own and in business for yourself in your own company, you are the owner. Your wealth will grow or shrink based on your success or failure.

Of course you'll have to work a lot, even more than as an employee. Forget the 9 to 5 workday, at least at the beginning. You will have all the responsibility of the company on your shoulders. This is one point many entrepreneurs overlook. They have to handle ALL aspects of the business, from creating the products and services, to winning new business, to doing the work, to handling the administration tasks. Of course, these days there are many people you could hire on a freelance basis to help you, but this depends on you, your business and the amount of working capital you have to pay fees to service providers.

Since you run the entire company, you will be the CEO, general manager, accountant, salesperson, computer technician, and receptionist all in one! Especially at the beginning of your business.

Be prepared. You will definitely become disappointed, frustrated or depressed at times. But as soon as your business gets off the ground, you will be very proud of yourself, extremely excited and free of any hierarchy.

Of course, sustainable success won't happen overnight. You may need a year, or even two or three, to see beginning of your results and success. But what a great feeling to do what you like. As an entrepreneur, working for yourself will motivate you more than anything else.

As a business owner, you are now the decision maker; there's no need to call your boss and ask permission to do something. You can try a new product or service, test a new model or variation. It's all up to you.

You no longer have to field disappointing remarks from your boss, such as "Thank you for your idea, but we have other plans." For me this aspect of being in my own business is priceless and that is my freedom. And at the same time, you don't have to rely on only yourself to make all the decisions in your business. You can, and should, hire freelance outside advisors to help you out. I explain this in detail in Chapter 10.

As an entrepreneur, you'll never have to gather your courage to ask for a raise. Although if you don't earn enough money to pay yourself, you can't ask anyone for an advance on your salary either!

If you plan and work efficiently in your business, you should be able to enjoy yourself, make more money, see your business grow and then make even more money.

Assuming you provide products or services that are valued by your target market, you'll become recognized and respected for your skills and the value you provide. People will pay you for your skills and your services. Before when you worked for your former employer, you were paid $25 per hour when he charged his customers $75 per hour, for example. As an entrepreneur you can charge your customers $60 or even $75 per hour and the profits are yours to earn and yours to keep.

As you create more and more value for your customers, you will become a recognized expert in your field; you will be respected and admired and people will listen to you.

What a feeling!

This new venture will be a great challenge, not an easy one, and along the way you will probably have some disappointment and rainy days for sure, but you will accomplish a great challenge.

To assist you in putting your ideas together, the next chapters will show you the steps to start and grow your business.

CHAPTER 2
The 12 Most Common Mistakes New Entrepreneurs Make

1. Not Knowing Whether You Like the Business Enough to Spend Morning, Noon and Night Working On It

My business, Biba4Network, is successful because it grew out of market demand as well as a personal need. I believe in the concept of networking and enjoy helping people. I needed a group like this when I started my US business and I couldn't find one. So I created the kind of group I required when I decided to start my own business in New York. Biba4Network is a natural outgrowth of my personal experiences and need.

I enjoy meeting people and helping them start businesses so they can succeed. And, I believe I am doing good things. As a result, the business is more of a personal mission to help people rather than a "business" or solely an income stream.

In addition, I have observed and counseled many entrepreneurs who embarked on a new venture because they wanted to be in business for themselves, rather than starting their own company because they wanted to help people or enjoyed the actual activities associated with the business. These people often failed because they weren't truly interested in the business or vested in the mission; they were more interested in making money.

2. Failing to Determine if the Business Actually Adds Value

The most sustainable businesses, those that withstand the test of time, provide value by performing a needed service and helping people.

For example, perhaps your accountant prepares your income tax return and also gives you advice that helps you reduce your tax liability. We could easily conclude that the accountant provides value. As a client, you may decide that the accountant's fees exceed the value of the services. While that accountant may be out of your price range, he/she still provides value.

3. Failing to Gain a Complete and Total Understanding of the Business

Every business has drivers, hot buttons, and key levers. What causes the business to succeed? What would make the business fail?

What drivers exist in your business?

Many business leaders, executives, and management consultants would say that success depends in a large part on attention to detail.

4. Inability to Describe the Business in Only One or Two Sentences

No doubt you've met the entrepreneur who thinks his business is so technical or complex he's unable to explain the concept in plain English. Or he takes 20 minutes to convey the purpose of the business.

Don't let this be you! In Chapter 12, you will learn how to describe your business and create an effective "elevator pitch."

5. Conducting Only Basic Research *(Or None At All)*

There are many great ideas you can latch on to, but the key in business is to make that sure the central theme or mission of your business venture can attract customers and generate sales and profits.

Some people want to be in business so badly they don't do their homework. They don't take the time to gain experience, study the business, understand what makes the business work, how to serve the customers and generate profits, and what leads to sales.

Often, this group's enthusiasm gets the better of them and as a result, they don't plan anything and never make a business plan.

It is of the utmost importance to make sure the market is big enough. In other words, assure there are enough target customers who will buy your products and services so you will bring in enough money to generate a profit.

Study your competitors; learn how you can improve upon their successes and avoid their failures and weaknesses. Discover why your competitors are valued by their customers. Develop a plan and design how you will differentiate yourself and your business in the marketplace.

A great idea in and of itself is not enough to start a business.

6. Failing to Contact Professionals & Established Experts Who Can Help You Started

Get a mentor or two. Surround yourself with experts who possess the skills and expertise you lack. If you are a marketing expert, you probably aren't an accountant or lawyer. Maybe you lack the skills to source your product. Team up with professionals who can complement your strengths and cover for your weaknesses.

I have counseled numerous entrepreneurs who believe only they can make their business a success. And I have worked with others who are afraid to spend money. As a result, they often fail because they don't get the sound advice and input they need which would have helped them avoid pitfalls and problems and become a success.

Many people ask their friends and family how to get started in business. The problem is that they often ask people who've never started or run a successful business. These people are not in a position to offer sound advice! If your uncle has never started a business most likely he doesn't have the hands-on experience to help you become a success in your new venture. How can he give you the right advice?

Even if you have to pay for professional advice to start your business and ensure your success, you will save time and money in the long run, as well as increase the likelihood you will succeed.

7. Raising or Allocating Inadequate Capital to the Business

- Do you know how much capital you need to start your business?
- Do you know your target market(s)?
- Did you calculate your costs and expenses?
- Did you project your sales?
- Do you know the number of clients you need to breakeven (to recover your costs) and the number of clients you need to reach your profit target?
- Do you know how much time you will have to allocate toward operating the business?
- Do you know how long it will take before you get your first benefits (health, dental, retirement, etc.) or how long you can sustain yourself and your family before you will run out of money?
- Do you know how many months you can pay your living expenses if your business takes longer than expected to generate a profit?

Invest the time to work on ALL aspects of your business before you start.

Above all else, take the time to work on your business plan. Without fail, create a written business plan!

8. Under-Budgeting for Marketing Costs

The world is overcrowded with businesses. Probably a number of those in your market perform essentially the same functions you do. This means you have to differentiate by making your business stand out.

Let's say that your business is writing and you've just published your first book. The typical huge bookstore carries 125,000 to 200,000 titles. How will you get YOUR book noticed? Can you expect to compete against Anthony Robbins? Robert Kiyosaki? T. Harv Eker? Brian Tracy? Mark Victor Hansen?

- Have you crafted a strategy to put the word out?
- Have you developed a plan to publicize your business and create awareness?
- Do you have plan for your sales, marketing, and publicity efforts?
- How much are you willing to spend on marketing your book?
- Who is your target reader and how can you reach them?

Marketing is key to any business (or book launch!)

Even if you start the business by yourself and don't plan to hire people at first this is the first category in which you will have to spend money. Publicity is essential to your livelihood; otherwise you will not attract any customers.

9. Failing to Make Marketing a Priority

Marketing should be one of your top priorities, particularly when you start your business, but in actuality, it should be a priority every day going forward.

It is essential you dedicate a good portion of your time and energy to working on and implementing your marketing plan.

Your marketing plan should be different from your business plan. Having a marketing plan means that you know exactly how to promote your products and services, and that you will have a system that will generate more clients for you.

10. Wanting to Market to Everybody

Once you develop your product or service, and perfect your offering you may think your offering is the best in your marketplace. This is especially likely if you are a highly confident person and created your business to serve an unmet need in your marketplace.

- While your products and services may be the best of the best, are you sure they are for everybody?
- Can you market a product or service to everybody?
- Does one size, in fact, really fit all?

Instead, carefully determine your niche, select a specific target market or market segment, and stick to it. You will have a more efficient message and achieve success much sooner.

11. Failing to Focus on the Business

Many entrepreneurs are energetic and enthusiastic people, but also overly optimistic and pursue too many targets and directions at once. This typically results in mediocre results. Define your business' mission as succinctly and narrowly as possible. Be practical! You can branch out and expand once you achieve some success.

When you move in too many directions at once, especially in the early days of your business, you are likely to fail to execute anything correctly. So you end up working "on the business" instead of "in the business."

This means you will spend all your time operating each task on your own. You won't have time to sit back and decide the best way to develop your own marketing plan, create new products, or improve your services. So in the end, you won't grow your business.

12. Failing to Follow-up with Clients

Many new entrepreneurs are so desperate to find new clients all the time they neglect the clients they already have. Statistics show it takes seven more interactions to secure a new client than to sell more to a repeat client. So develop and maintain a useful and organized follow-up system to offer new services to your clients and don't let them slip away.

With proper planning, thorough adaptation, and solid implementation you will be much more likely to succeed. This does not mean you'll automatically avoid making mistakes or missteps or you'll always realize a significant return on your investment. But it can mean you will be much more likely to succeed, to generate a profit, and to build a sustainable business for the long haul.

CHAPTER 3
6 Easy Ways to Start Your Business & Avoid Those 12 Mistakes

1. Brainstorm your Ideas from Top to Bottom and Left to Right, and Set a Plan

Be sure to set goals and milestones and attach firm deadlines to the milestones. Milestones are key steps along the path towards establishing your business. These key steps will help you focus your energies and stay on track to create your successful business.

By defining the key ingredients or action steps you must accomplish to get your business up and running, and putting a deadline on each step, you increase the likelihood ten or twenty fold that you will succeed.

Since I started my first business in 1998 I have met lot of people, including friends, who often tell me, "You're so lucky, you have your own business, you do what you love; I should do it too."

I always answer, "So do it!"

Without exception, each person proceeds to raise their objections and limitations, "Well this isn't easy. I won't have a paycheck anymore. What if I can't get clients at first? What if I can't pay my rent? What business is best suited for me? I have some ideas, but I am not sure whether they're right for me or whether I can earn a living."

Despite my success, level of self-confidence, and the fact that I quit my job on a Friday night to start my business on Monday morning, I was scared when I started my new business. And even after achieving success in my business in France, I started again from scratch in the United States, a foreign country to me. I was still scared.

But I prevailed, and SO CAN YOU.

The secret to success in any endeavor is to commit and devote your energies and total focus to the initiative. You must take some risks and put yourself into the fray. This is the only way you will get what you want.

If you feel more comfortable, start your business part-time, so you'll feel secure you still have a paycheck until your business generates enough money for you to leave your job.

Wanting to be an entrepreneur is really great but those goals and dreams are not enough to guarantee your success. To become a successful entrepreneur, you must know exactly what you are going to do, both when and how. In other words, you must have a crystal clear, specific product offering, as well as a path and method of implementation.

So that is definitely the first step.

What do you enjoy doing in your life, in your spare time, or as a hobby? Is there any way to turn this into a business?

- What do you like to do?
- What activities do you excel at?
- What are your strengths?
- What skills, insights, expertise, know-how, and interests do you possess that will enable you to deliver valuable products or services to your target market?

Take a pen and a paper and put your ideas in writing. When you commit your thoughts to paper, you will have a blueprint, a way to refine your thinking, and ask yourself the tough questions. Once you commit your thoughts and ideas to paper, analyze each idea in terms of benefits or rewards, and risks and pitfalls. On one side of the page, list the positive factors and on the other, the negative factors.

Then for each idea, ask yourself the following questions:
- What if this doesn't succeed; do I have a back-up?
- What could go wrong?
- How much money do I need to start?
- Who could I ask for advice?
- Do I need a partner or can I do it on my own?
- How will I operate?
- How will I deliver the product or service?
- What do I need to do to deliver superior customer satisfaction?
- What do I need to do to buy the product?
- Where can I find supplies?
- How is the market in that field? Do I know the market?

This analysis will give you a better idea of what you would like to do or what you need to do to organize your interests as a business.

Actually, that was the easy part; now you will have to develop your idea, which means you have to start your business plan.

2. Craft Your Business Plan and Perfect It

Writing a business plan is the most important step in the process of starting your own business venture. In many ways, your ability to organize your business and move from the concept stage to the implementation to breakeven to profit depends on the quality of your business plan and the degree to which you implement your plan successfully.

Your business plan does not have to be a novel. But it must be clear and to-the-point. The more you can use the document as a "thinking tool," the more benefit you'll derive from the exercise.

Refer to Chapter 4 to learn in detail how to write your business plan

3. Organize Your Finances

Once you have your business plan, you will have a clearer idea of what your business will be like and what actions you must take to succeed. The next step is to create a budget to determine how much capital you will need to start your business and what the economics of the business are likely to be. Answer the following questions:

- How much capital do you need to start your business?
- How much money will you need before you breakeven?
- How much time will you need before you start generating enough funds to cover some of your living expenses? All of your living expenses?
- Do you have the money you need to get started?
- Do you need to raise money from investors or borrow money from a lender?
- Do you have enough personal savings to cover your living expenses until your business can generate an income for you?

Depending on the size of your project, I suggest that first you look around you for sources of capital.

Do you have savings?

Even though I started my first business with no savings whatsoever, I really recommend that you have at least three to six months of savings to cover your living expenses before your start your business.

Can you borrow money to your friends and family?

If you don't require too much capital, it could be a good idea to use your own savings or borrow money from your friends or family members. Although there could be other risks attached to this path.

To avoid these risks, handle the transaction professionally. If you borrow money from friends or family, sign a loan agreement with them. State when you plan to repay the money, agree on a timeframe, and make sure you will respect the agreement. In the event you have to go beyond that period of time, add an addendum or amendment to your agreement.

I borrowed money from my parents on two occasions, and I always wrote a loan agreement. Even though they always said, "You can give us the money back when you want or when you can" or "We don't need the money back; that is part of your inheritance anyway," I always said, "No, we must sign a loan agreement." Even if your lender ultimately waives the requirement to repay the loan, the mere existence of the contract gives you discipline and adds professionalism to the entire process.

Trust me, when the day comes when you finish repaying that loan and you sign the final release letter that acknowledges you paid the loan, you will feel SO GOOD and SO PROUD. And you should!

Yes, you accepted their help to start, but at the end when you don't owe any money to anybody, you know that you did all of this on your own. That is your success to enjoy and cherish and nobody else's.

If you don't have friends or family who can help you with your start-up, you can look for investors or bank loans. It is very important that you develop a strong relationship with your bank or banker since they will be your "partner."

4. Protect Yourself

This is also a very important step. When you start your own business, you must protect yourself, your business and your assets. Today, people are quick to sue and a loss could wipe out your assets.

Many people start their business as a sole proprietorship, which is probably the easiest and least expensive way to start a business, but that doesn't give you any significant legal protection.

Your financing need for outside capital will influence the legal structure you select. That is why I counsel each new business owner that they first need to consult with a lawyer AND an accountant before they decide which business structure is best for them. Then, and only then, when you have ALL the information you need, you can incorporate.

In addition to the form of legal entity you select, you must obtain adequate insurance coverage. There are all types of coverage you may need depending on your business. For example, professional liability, product liability, and office insurance are just a few of the types of insurance that you may need. Consult your insurance broker.

5. Your First Steps as a Small Business Owner

Now that you made the decision to start your business, developed your ideas, created your business plan, and identified or raised financing, where will you work?

In other words, where will you establish your place of business?

- Do you need an office?
- Will you work from home?
- Can you use your garage or a portion of your basement?
- Do you have all the supplies you need?
- Are your phone lines, Internet access and fax working?
- Will you be the one who will pick up the phone, or do you need a receptionist?

6.Your Marketing Plan?

As mentioned earlier, many small business owners want to start their own business so badly, that they skip the process of developing their marketing strategy.

- Do you have professional materials: business cards, a logo, brochure, and website?
- Do you know how to introduce your product or service?
- Have you developed and practiced your elevator pitch to introduce yourself and promote yourself to potential clients? (Refer to Chapter 12 to learn how to create an effective elevator pitch)
- Do you know where and how to get your first clients?
- Do you have a marketing plan to communicate with your prospects and clients?
- Have you planned all of this before you meet your first prospect?

Statistics show that people make their buy/no-buy decision in the first 10 seconds or less, so don't miss your opportunity to make that key first impression. Be ready! Get going!

CHAPTER 4
Why You Need a Business Plan

Starting a business is exciting and exhilarating. When your business plan addresses many of the key points concerning the business and the "what ifs" then you will significantly increase your probability of success. The quality of your business plan will greatly impact the future and success of your business.

Your business plan helps you plan your activities and focus your efforts for the next few years. You need to spend a significant amount of time developing your business plan to ensure that you provide all the information, questions, and solutions that will help you start your business and make it a success.

Here are a handful of other reasons why you need a business plan: to clarify your goals, to estimate how much money you need to get started, to source the resources you need to implement your plan, to obtain a loan from a bank, to attract investment capital from investors, to support an immigration visa application, to track your business' progress, and to help you attract customers and vendors.

You'll find a number of business plan templates available on the Internet. You can use those samples, but make sure to adapt them to your business. The most important point is to be clear and concise. Your business plan could be between 20 to 40 pages long but the quality of the thought process and information is much more important than the length.

One of the important parts of your business plan is your financial projections and sales. This is the amount of goods and services you will sell and at what price. It's useful to consider the timing. The financial projections should also include realistic estimates of the costs and expenses you will incur to start and run your business. Again, spend enough time researching your industry and competitors to find out the real potential and the realistic costs of your business.

Your business plan should also include your mission statement, your business strategy, research on your target market and your target customers' demographics, industry analysis (size, economics, trends, success factors, challenges, etc.), your marketing plan, your suppliers, and operating licenses if needed.

Here are some questions your business plan can help you answer:
- Who are your competitors?
- What makes your competitors successful?
- What makes you unique compared to the competition?
- Who is your target market?
- How you will promote your products or services?
- How will you reach your clients?
- What marketing techniques can you implement that will help you create awareness and effectively promote your products and services to your target customers?
- What is a reasonable price range for your products or services?
- How will you source products or services?
- Will you need to hire employees? What will they do?
- How much will they cost in terms of wages and benefits?

All of these elements will help you to determine how much investment you will need to start your business, when you will break-even, and when you will realize profits.

I recommend you create a detailed business plan; this will help you make informed decisions about your business.

I find it's better to know all the aspects of the business up front rather than discovering the pitfalls after you invest your money, time, and energy. While it is impossible to forecast and address every single issue you will face, with the right detail and research effort, you will be able to highlight and address many of the issues you are likely to face.

I've worked with some entrepreneurs who started their businesses without a business plan and then realized they couldn't operate the business effectively, didn't enjoy the business, lacked the required skills to excel or the interest to master the subject matter, and realized they didn't have the financial strength or capital that was required to make the business a success.

Many entrepreneurs write their business plans themselves, while others hire consultants to help them craft the plan from start to finish. In any case, a business plan will help you develop your business strategies and tactics and give you greater confidence to progress and succeed.

Since you will submit your business plan to others, like to banks and investors, who will use your plan to evaluate your business, it is important that your plan be well-written, thorough and sensible. Make sure to contact editors, consultants, and other professionals to review your document before you present it to a bank or investor.

If you will be making a face-to-face presentation, be sure to rehearse your speech so you will be very comfortable and confident when making your presentation to a professional audience.

The time you invest in crafting, reviewing and practicing your business plan is time well spent. These efforts will force you to carefully analyze your business and decide whether this is something you truly want to do.

When you start your business, your business plan can serve as a guide and solutions manual. Over time, you will need to update the plan, perhaps every quarter, but not less than once a year.

CHAPTER 5
Identifying Your Ideal Client

In order to help your clients and fulfill their needs you first need to know exactly who your ideal clients are. What do they really want and need? It's very important to stop and think for a moment to answer this big question: "Who are your ideal clients?"

Do you really want to chase everyone or do you have a specific niche? Realistically, no business can serve everyone and no product or service is right for everyone. When you have a clear idea of who your ideal clients are you'll know your niche.

Many new small business owners are so afraid to lose a sale that they market their products so "wildly" and aggressively that sometimes the client can't even see, recognize, or tell if the product is a good fit for him or her. Or if he or she will benefit from using the product or service.

If you try to sell your products or services to everybody, you're not only losing time and opportunity, you're also losing big money.

Your ideal customers...
- Who are they? Who are you targeting?
- Are they men, women, teenagers, children, seniors, individuals, corporations, entrepreneurs, etc. How would you describe, in just a few words your ideal target market?

- What are the demographics?
    - How old are they?
    - Should you target everybody or a range of people?
    - Where do they live?
    - Should your message be the same if they are located in big cities or small towns?
- Where are they located?
    - Do you know where to find them?
    - Can you join the same groups and organizations?
    - Do you know what publications they read so you can advertise in their favorite magazines?
- Do you know where they go to buy products that are similar to yours?

Make it easy for your target customers to find you. If you know exactly what they need, it will be easier for you to adapt your products and services to provide them with the right offering, the right package of features and benefits. Be as specific as you can so your marketing message will get right to the point and reach your target market.

- What do they want or need?
- What are the biggest challenges and obstacles in their lives or businesses?

See yourself as a problem solver; what can you offer them and how?

If you are reading this book now and never really ask yourself these questions, it is time to write down both the questions and the answers right now. The best way to start is to look at your current actual clients, what they have in common and how you can determine a profile of your ideal clients.

Let's go back to profile your ideal clients:

Who are your ideal clients?

What are their demographics?

Where are they?

What do they want and need?

What are the biggest challenges in their lives and businesses?

How can you solve their problems?

Now that you know who your ideal clients are your next question is: How will you market your business and offering to attract more and more customers?

PART II
Strategies to
Grow Your Business

CHAPTER 6
How to Position &
Price Your Services

Pricing goods and services can be complex. There are many pricing strategies and methods; often the pricing efforts require both creativity and experimentation. Over the years, I have worked with business who priced their products and services at an amount that barely exceeded their costs and yielded relatively low profit margins.

During the process of crafting your business plan and studying your competitors, evaluate the price ranges your competition offers, as well as the policies they follow.

As a general rule of thumb, position yourself in the upper end of the range. This assumes numerous people offer the same or similar products and services and the offerings are not identical. By setting your prices in the upper portion of the overall price range in your market conveys a sense of quality and status.

Depending on your profit margins, you may have the flexibility to negotiate on price with your customers. If you set your prices too low, you are likely to get squeezed on price. Companies who price their services at "bargain levels" often find that they cannot deliver high quality because in order to generate a profit, they need to skimp on materials, hire less costly or less experienced labor, or spend fewer hours than is realistically required in order to control labor costs.

Sound pricing strategy does not entail revealing to your clients that you charge lower rates than your competitors. It does entail educating your clients about the benefits you offer.

Basically, your prices should be high enough that you can pay your expenses and earn a "fair" profit for your investment of time, money and know-how.

"Fair" depends on the market. If you charge higher prices than any other provider in your marketplace, but your customers continue to hire you instead of the competition, your customers most likely believe you provide great value, especially compared to the competition.

Pricing considerations include:
- How much it costs to operate your business
- Your profit targets
- The image you want your business to create in the customers' minds
- How much your customers are willing to pay for your offering
- How much the competition is charging (prices and pricing levels)
- The degree to which customers can substitute a competitor's products and services for yours
- Traditional standards in your marketplace and your ability to change or break from tradition
- Your evaluation, based on research, experience and instinct, of what price levels the market will accept

The first step is to figure out how much money you need to collect in order to breakeven; how many units of product or hours of service you require to cover your costs and reach your profit goals. This is known as a "Breakeven Analysis" and provides data that can help you determine the likelihood you will succeed in your business.

To calculate your breakeven point make sure to include all your costs, including goods, sales needs, office and administrative fees, taxes, etc.

Divide your costs into two categories: variable and fixed costs.

1. Variable costs change in relation to production volume or the quantity of goods and services you sell.
2. Fixed costs remain constant across certain ranges or a volume of business activity.

Calculate the breakeven point with the following equation:

Breakeven point = Fixed Costs divided by Gross Profit.

Fixed costs = those costs and expenses that you incur regardless of the number of customers you serve or the quantity of product you sell.

Variable costs = the total costs during the period that change in relation to the volume of business activity.

With this information, you can determine how much sales revenue you need to generate to recover all your costs. If you want to generate a certain target profit you can add the dollar profit target to your fixed costs. You can also analyze the impact on required sales quantity from raising or lowering your prices, and the results of increased or decreased sales.

Suppose your operating costs are relatively high compared to your competitors. One example is two restaurants that serve the same food. Assume Bob's rent is $3,000 per month while Jane's rent is only $1,500 per month. Bob has higher cost base and will have a more difficult time earning a profit than Jane. By examining the number of meals Bob needs to sell and the prices he has to charge in order to generate a profit, Bob can estimate if his business is viable.

Research your market and determine your pricing strategy and make the right decisions about your business. Don't forget, you can always adjust your rates over time!

CHAPTER 7
How to Attract More Clients &
Close More Sales

If you already own your own business but haven't achieved the results you expected, or if you are just starting out, here are three ways to grow your business.

1. Attract more clients
2. Increase your prices
3. Increase how often your clients buy from you

1. Attract more clients

Depending on the products or services that you offer, there are different tactics to use to expand your client roster.
Ask yourself:
- Why you don't close more sales?
- Do you make enough sales calls?
- Do you call on the right people? (People who are likely to be interested in your products and services?)
- Are your prospects afraid to buy from you because of the risk they will take with the product or service itself or because they don't know you yet?

Today, people are often skeptical. When you reduce the risk of making a purchase from your business, you will create an environment that allows people to buy more from you and buy more often than they otherwise would have.

It is very important you build a relationship with your prospects, leads, and customers so they will trust you, conduct business with you and buy from you.

How can you break their fears?

By offering a sample of your product, you can create a great opportunity for people to test your products and services before they make the decision to buy from you.

Have you noticed companies that advertise on TV? Very often you will see an invitation to "Call for your free brochure," or "Call to receive a free sample."

Why do you think these merchants pay a lot of money (I mean millions of dollars) to advertise on TV plus pay more to send you a sample? Because they know they may give away a certain number of products but they'll earn a return on their investment.

In other words, by putting the product into the target customer's hands, they create a relationship with the customer. They provide incentives for customers to test their products, and see the results for themselves. This is a proven way to build your customer base and increase sales.

Probably a number of people will only take the free sample and never make a purchase, but the merchant also gains the opportunity to sell products to people who would never buy if they didn't try it for free first. Those people may become repeat customers.

If nothing else, the merchant builds his or her mailing list. This can be especially valuable since most of the people who request the sample are interested in the product. They're the ideal target market. And even though a portion of the respondents will not make a purchase right away, they may make a purchase in the future.

What if your products or services can't be sold as a sample?

Well, be creative. Let's say you offer a free report, a e-book, or booklet to give your target clients. In your publication, you provide information about your products and services. They'll learn more about you, which will position you as an expert in your field, and a good percentage of those people will be more willing to contact you instead of your competitor when they need this product or service.

Take my Free mini e-course at www.TheConnectionQueen.com as an example. Sending 15 networking tips in 15 days helps people answer their questions, but also learn more about me, who I am, and how I can help them.

Similar, in one of my other businesses, MyFrenchNetwork.com, I offer a consultation for people who want to start a business. Being able to speak with the potential client and answer all of his or her questions helps me to learn more about their projects. I can give them advice, show them how I can help them, and more importantly build a relationship with them.

This example is the best way to show you how people contact you, instead of contacting them, to try to sell them something.

In www.MyFrenchNetwork.com just giving access to lots of information on my website, plus offering a free consultation, means I have 4 to 5 people calling me every week. After the consultation, 80% become clients immediately, 10% contact me within few months when they are ready to launch their business, and 10% don't become clients. The 10% don't become clients either because they give up on their business or don't have the finances to start. Regardless, they still receive my newsletter on a regular basis and I communicate with them; this means the day they are ready, I'll be on their mind and they'll come to me.

When people meet you they'll see you know what you're talking about and that you have the expertise and knowledge to help them. They'll realize there is a "real person" behind your brochure or website. And if you can give them valuable information during this consultation, they'll be more willing to start working with you and buy from you when they are ready.

Implement this strategy on your business and you will be surprised on how you will easily attract more clients.

Another simple way to deliver your expertise for free is to start an email newsletter or e-zine. You'll have an opportunity to demonstrate the advantages of your business on a regular basis as well as show people how you can help solve their problems and showcase the benefits of working with you. You'll learn more about this later on in this chapter.

Word of mouth referrals from satisfied customers is typically the best way to advertise and promote your business.

How do you do that?

Simply get testimonials from your current clients.

Contact your best clients; they already know you, appreciate and value your products and services. Most likely they will be happy to give you a testimonial that praises your products and services. Be sure to obtain their permission to use their information in your marketing. Also ask them for referrals: friends, colleagues or family who would benefit from your products also.

Then prepare a direct mail campaign. Don't you think that when the targets see their friends' names in your brochure that they will establish trust with you and break their fear? You will get a better response to your campaign than advertising in a magazine where nobody knows you and most readers won't even notice your ad.

When you start a business, you have to spend your money wisely so it is very important to do some homework first.

Make sure your message is clear and well-targeted.

Use strong headlines to grab your prospects' attention. Just as a recruiter spends only few seconds reading your resume when you look for a job, a prospect will take a quick look at your brochure. If nothing grabs his attention within a few seconds, he'll discard it. What a waste of time and money!

But when you know how to choose the right headlines, the right words, the right tagline, and if you know how to grab their interest within the first lines and show how your products and services can benefit them, they will read your entire brochure and order.

In your conclusion you'll offer them a great opportunity they can't miss and motivate them to take action now and contact you; you'll realize a high return on your campaign. Again, not everybody will contact you, but you'll achieve a better result than just placing an ad in a newspaper and waiting by your phone for people to contact you.

While crafting the right campaign for your market: the right message, the right format, and the right offer, the only way you'll be able to gauge your results is by measuring your marketing promotion or campaign. Include a "call to action" that creates a sense of urgency so people will act quickly and contact you.

Direct mail is often one of the most effective sales methods, yet creating and implementing a campaign can be expensive. In addition to buying or renting a mailing list, you have to design and print the materials. Direct mail packages typically include a sales letter, often a brochure, a business reply envelope, PLUS the original mailing. And of course there's the postage!

The direct sales industry considers a 2% response rate for a direct mail piece to be a success. Depending on the price of your product or service to earn a decent living you'll have to mail a huge quantity of packages.

The wisest way to proceed is to start slowly, on a small scale, and test the effectiveness of your message. Craft a message and send it to 100 prospects. Consider crafting a second message and sending that to a different 100 prospects. The best way to test your results is to change only one item in each package at a time. When you change multiple items in the package at once, it's impossible to determine which item accounts for the results.

You can track results by coding your response card or offer. This means you'll create a series of "promotion codes" and when a person responds to the offer you'll capture the response code so you can collect statistics.

The complete direct mail package includes a message that ends with an offer, a call to action, a deadline, and your contact information. Be clear in what you want them to do in your call to action; the prospect must know what to do when they receive your information. Do you want them to call you? Send you an email? Return the postcard? Make a purchase?

Using the profile of your ideal clients we studied earlier, be creative and find new ideas to reach them.

Did you ever receive emails from companies that were ready to offer you a CD, book, or a movie ticket in exchange for the names of five of your friends? I have. A couple of years ago, I received four free movie tickets just for forwarding an email to my friends. They got free tickets too and then thanked me. Everybody was happy, including the company running this campaign, because they were able to build their mailing list.

Whatever you do, you always have to think how to attract clients instead of waiting for them to find you.

2. Raise the prices of your products or services

Another way to grow your business when you're established or have been in business for a few months is to raise the price of your products and services.

If you're like many entrepreneurs, when you started your business you probably wanted to sell to everybody. I did this, too. You want to make sure you don't lose any sales and you may even be ready to lower your prices to ensure you'll close the sale. But after a while you realize you're working a lot for very little money, you're not breaking even, and you're actually losing money. So this is clearly not the best technique.

It's not easy to say "no" to a client; we always think if we say "no" they'll never buy again or they'll run to the competitor. Some of them might but let your competitors lose money; you have other goals.

When you've been in business for a while, you'll be more comfortable with your products and services; you'll be more comfortable with yourself; you'll gain greater self-confidence, and you'll develop the courage to raise your prices. As long as you provide great customer service, have testimonials from a number of satisfied clients, and know that there is value in what you offer, there's no reason to lower your prices.

Of course you won't raise your price by 50% at one time but you can add more value to your products and services in order to justify the price increase. You can develop different levels and bundles of services or packages.

Photographers often offer two or three different packages of their services. They offer the basic package at an entry rate but if you want more photos you can purchase the premium package or the deluxe package. The multiple offering makes it easier for the client to make a purchase according to his or her budget and interests.

It is easy, simple, and there is no discussion over price. You buy what you want and you get what you buy.

Many coaches and consultants also use this technique because it's a way to avoid negotiating or arguing over the price of the service. Instead of speaking about price they can ask their prospect, "What program are you interested in?" This helps you avoid mentioning the words "price" and "dollar" which tend to scare people. If selling isn't your favorite part of the business or you don't like to speak about money, practice your offering until you become comfortable. You'll achieve better results if you sound confident.

Even if you lose some clients because you increase your prices, that's not necessarily a bad thing. You will have fewer clients but earn more money for your time and services, as well as work less, which will give you more time to work on your own marketing plan to grow your business or more time for yourself.

If you are really worried about losing too many clients, apply your new rates only to new clients. Wait for the New Year, a seasonal change, or natural "deadline" in your industry to raise your rates to your current clients, little by little.

Consider this: if you had to choose one option but knew both options would work in your marketplace, which would you prefer:

- 20 clients a month x $299 = $5,980
- 40 clients a month x $149 = $5,960

I would definitely choose the first option!

Take the time to see how you can add value to your products or services and apply this to your business.

Of course this will not happen overnight. Here's the technique I used to progressively raise my prices; it will give you some ideas on how you can raise your prices to grow and boost your business as well.

When I started Biba4Network the business of networking was a new world for me, and I didn't really know what to charge for an event. I looked at my competitors and charged less. (I told you that I made the underpricing my services mistake too!) I thought if I was less expensive than the competition, more people would attend my events.

I quickly realized my attendance wasn't higher just because I was less expensive than other networking groups. After a few months, I raised the price from $15 to $25, which is the amount most networking groups charge for their events. I noticed I didn't have fewer people and I even found that more people attended the events. Why? Often higher prices create the perception of greater value.

Then I started a membership program for $99 per year, which included admission to every event for free. A few months later, I kept the $99 membership fee but since I was holding more and more events, I required members to pay $10 per event or they could bring a guest and attend free. This option gave them a choice, and at the same time generated more exposure for me and expanded my network.

The "bring a friend" campaign encouraged my existing members to promote my company and my events, all by word of mouth. Some of the guests eventually became members as well. That created and continues to create a win-win situation.

Later I began offering a "VIP Membership" for $249; VIP members could attend all the events for free. So again people had a choice; I didn't push one or the other; they chose what level was right for them I found that more and more people were joining at the VIP level.

Then I raised the $99 per a year plus $10 per event to $149 per a year plus $10 per event. Why? Because I knew my service was working and my members were getting positive results. More and more members were getting valuable referrals and clients through my events and network. They were successfully growing their businesses.

But I didn't just raise the prices; I added value to the package: a new service, an online community where members could exchange and network with other members, etc. This created a new opportunity for my members to network between meetings, spend more time learning about each other, and accelerated the process to get to know each other. They were better able to help each other, develop trust and friendships, and do business with each other.

I actually started selling consulting services to help people start and grow their businesses for $99. Less than a year later, with a lot more confidence because of the results I had with clients and great testimonials, I raised the price to $1,000 for my consulting services. Today those services sell for $11,000 and include tons of value.

I did the exact same thing in my coaching business. My prices started very low but with more experience and expertise, I raised my prices. Today I'm able to help most of my clients to double or triple their revenues within 2 to 3 months and my private clients pay me thousands of dollars to access my business building strategies.

It isn't difficult to raise your prices as long as you offer a useful product or service and people can see the value in your offering. Your ability to raise your prices will vary depending on your market but it's worthwhile to test your pricing and your offering. Customers will be willing to pay more when they know the quality they'll receive from you and understand the benefits for them.

3. Increase how often your clients buy from you

Statistics reveal that it's much more difficult to close a new client than to keep an existing one. So why do most business owners still spend most of their marketing budget looking for new clients? Don't get me wrong; I am not saying you shouldn't look for new clients. You do need to cultivate new clients on a regular basis. But are you missing opportunities to sell more products and services to your current client base?

When people are already your clients and are satisfied with your products and services, don't you think they'll buy again? They trust you. I mentioned this before: clients who have already bought from you will be more willing to buy from you again than new customers who don't know you yet and have never bought from you.

So of course your clients are likely to buy again but if they never hear from you, chances are that they will try something else. Your customers are bombarded with thousands of daily messages from TV and radio commercials, newspaper and magazine ads, billboards, Internet banners, emails, and more. If you don't keep in contact with them, they'll forget about you or be tempted by a free offer I mentioned in Chapter 9.

CHAPTER 8
Staying Connected to Your Clients & Prospects

Make sure you constantly and consistently communicate with your current clients. You'll put forth less far effort to "sell" your existing clients than to convert your new prospects into new customers. You'll close more sales from your existing clients because they'll become repeat clients. Don't make the mistake of forfeiting "easy" sales. Keep in touch with your clients on a regular basis.

One of the easiest ways to keep in touch with your existing clients, and help newcomers get to know you, is to start an email newsletter or e-zine. Publishing an e-zine won't cost you much and you can send a message every month, twice a month, or every week, depending on how much you have to say and how often you want to connect with your clients and prospects.

I send my newsletter every Friday morning. The newsletter informs my members and subscribers of up-coming events and also gives them articles from experts and valuable resources related for small business owners.

I noticed a number of people who've been in business for a year, two years, or more and still don't have a way to communicate with their clients or prospects. They have never built their mailing list and are surprised when they don't get more clients.

There are three simple things that I recommend and suggest to my clients who are ready to start their own business.

1. Order professional business cards

This helps to portray your business image and makes you stand out from the crowd. The card helps people you meet remember you and makes it easier for those people to contact you again, or to give your card to other people as a referral.

That is your first marketing tool that will make a difference. People tend to keep business cards in a business card file, book, or Rolodex®, or they enter the data in their electronic organizer.

2. Create a website

Even if you have only two or three pages to start! People need to find you and find out exactly who you are, what you do, and how they'll benefit from an association with you and your products and services.

3. Publish a newsletter

Most of my clients accept the first two ideas above but when it comes to publishing a newsletter they say, "Yes. Thank you. That is a good idea, but I just started my business, so what can I put in my newsletter?" They go on to worry about things like:

- How often do I send it?
- Who will read it?
- How do I publish it?
- Will it cost money?
- And so on.

You can launch your newsletter even before you start your business with a pre-opening introduction!

Initially, you can publish your newsletter once a month to describe your products or services, introduce yourself, and give your readers an opportunity to learn more about you. Right away, you'll start to build a relationship with them. You don't have to publish a very long newsletter; you can include a few important tips on your area of expertise, an article you've written, or even a reprint other people's articles. You need to communicate with your customers, prospects, and leads on a regular basis.

I started writing articles in French years ago and consistently publish one article per a month on my website, My French Network, and in my newsletter. But I wasn't ready to write in English yet so I started posting other people's articles related to my industry as resources for my readers. Of course never forget to ask permission to reprint an article!

Little by little, I wrote a short paragraph in English about myself so people would feel that they know me. Slowly I gained more confidence in writing and started publishing my newsletter in English.

This is funny now because when I meet people that I have never met before at networking events, often when they hear my name, they say: "Hey, you're Biba! I heard so much about you. I'm on your mailing list and I read your newsletter every week." Often it seems they already know everything about me.

When I meet people I first met years ago when I started my business, but didn't have the opportunity to see them again since that initial meeting, they congratulate me on how I grew my business since we met. How do they know that? They're on my mailing list!

Even if I haven't seen them in a while they still "hear" about me on a regular basis. When we meet again we aren't strangers. That helps because we don't need to reconnect and start the process of building trust and our relationship again; we already have a relationship. That's how I was able to partner with different people; they felt they already knew me for a period of time and developed trust.

To answer the question, "Who will read it?" it's easy. Ask everybody you know if you can put them on your mailing list. Explain how often you'll mail them and how they can opt-out. Be sure to ask their permission; you never want to be accused of spam or junk mail!

Put a box on your website where people can subscribe to your mailing list. This is another reason why your website is so important! Don't let you reader leave your website without signing up for your newsletter. Mention your newsletter each time you meet somebody and tell them the benefits they'll receive when they sign-up: free information, tips, or special offers. That is how you'll build and grow your list.

I first built my mailing list by adding everybody I met during networking events; mine events and others. After each networking event, or each time I met someone who gave me their business card, the next day I always sent them an email to mention it was a pleasure meeting them and I wanted to learn more about them and their business. I also asked if they would send me information or to add me to their newsletter. At the same time, I told them I would add them to my newsletter to help them learn more about my business and because I provide a lot of resources to help them grow their business.

Of course, I always mentioned that if they didn't enjoy the newsletter or didn't want to receive it anymore, they could remove their name and email address at any time. Surprisingly, very few people asked to be removed from the list. Within a few months, I collected hundreds of names and that's how my mailing list grew. Today I reach thousands of small business owners in the New York area and around the US as well as from other countries including France, Canada, England, and Australia. Just to name a few!

It's important you start your own newsletter as soon as possible. You'll be sure to reach your target market and for your special promotions you'll have a better return than if you just advertised in a newspaper.

Your newsletter is also the opportunity for you to send your message over and over again. And since we know that people need to see the same message at least seven times before they buy, your newsletter will cost you a lot less than if you run an ad in a newspaper seven times. Your newsletter will also give you the opportunity to offer special sales opportunities to your readers, which directly answers the question "How to increase the rate at which clients buy?"

CHAPTER 9
Using Your Newsletter to Close More Sales

You should take any opportunity to offer a special sale. When I was living in New York I was amazed by the number of "Special Sale Days" offered by major department stores! They always have a special: "Wednesday Sale: 50% Off" and two days later there's the "Weekend Special Sale – 60% to 70% Off".

Why not do the same to boost your sales? You don't have to have a physical store to hold a special sale! Take every occasion to give a special offer: a holiday sale, a Christmas sale, an after-Christmas sale, a Halloween sale, a Valentine's Day sale, a Spring sale, a Summer sale, a 50% off on your products, a Buy 1-Get 1 free offer, a special it's my Birthday celebration, and more! Over time, I have noticed many consultants and coaches use these techniques and many of these ideas work very well.

People like bargains. It's a chance for them to try your products they would probably never buy at full price. You may be thinking: "If I have a special sale all the time I'll lose money." The answer is NO! You'll sell more products and services than you usually do. You'll gain new customers and potential repeat customers so when you price your products and services properly, you will actually make more money.

A few years ago I read the story of a marketing consultant who tripled her revenue during the last week of December by offering 50% off on every one of her products. She sent three reminders to her newsletter subscribers, including one on December 31st. She was amazed by the results. When most people struggle to do business during the holidays, she actually sold more than during a regular month.

So guess what I did the next December? A holiday special sale! And the result? I tripled my revenue compared to the prior December.

One of the first books I read when I started my business in New York was Anthony Robbins' "Awaken the Giant Within: How to Take Immediate Control of Your Mental, Emotional, Physical, and Financial Destiny!" A friend of mine gave me the book.

I never heard about Anthony Robbins before; now he is one of my mentors. I really recommend his book. Among the different things that I learned from his book is that if you really want to succeed in life or in your business, there is no need to reinvent the wheel. Tony explains that, "You just have to choose a successful person in your field that you admire, watch what he or she is doing, do everything he or she is doing and you will be successful too." And it works.

Special offers will also give your inactive clients a reason to buy from you again and get back in touch. They bought from you at the regular price the first time, so perhaps they would love a bargain this time.

Follow up with your clients a couple of weeks after they bought from you. When you follow up, offer them another product! Statistics show up to one out of three clients will take advantage of this new offer. If you don't have another product or service to sell, partner with other businesses that have a product that complements your product. This is called an affiliate program.

The same concept applies when you recommend a book, movie, product, or service to a friend; they trust you and will buy because the information comes from you. The only difference with affiliate programs is that you get paid each time you make a sale.

There are a number of online directories for affiliate programs and many companies offer their own programs. But I have one rule: I only promote products from people I know personally and who are successful in their field. I like to promote products I use and find useful.

Affiliate programs are another way to make more revenue plus you'll have repeat clients! When you launch your own new product they'll be willing to buy again. In my case, I created a habit with my clients; I send them regular information and offers instead of waiting months for me to create my new own product.

As a conclusion of this chapter, I will add that it is essential to build a very, very special relationship with your clients. They are your best audience: they are the ones who sell for you when they recommend your products and services, when they testify how satisfied they are, how you help them or how you solve their problems. Plus, your loyal clients will be the best audience for your new products and services.

Just like a fan who buys every CD by his favorite singer or DVD featuring his favorite actor, your clients will buy from you again and again!

Treat your clients as your dear friends. Always give the best of you. As you've probably heard many times before: "Under Promise and Over Deliver." Guide them to take action, offer them your best deal, and always follow-up. Never neglect or overlook your current clients! Become part of their routine. If they hear from you regularly with a message, phone call, brochure, post-card, thank you note, birthday or holiday card you'll always be present in their mind when it comes time to refer you to others or when they need your products or services. If you miss that step you'll lose business.

CHAPTER 10
Why You Need a Team of Experts

Just because you own your own business doesn't mean you have to perform every task yourself. The world is so complicated it's impossible to know everything you need to do in your business. Even if you did, performing each and every task is a poor use of your time! In other words, you must prioritize and delegate.

Like most small business owners, you are definitely good at what you do. Who better than you knows your products or services? But are you a CPA? A lawyer? An advertising manager? A marketing consultant? A webmaster? A secretary? Probably not.

When you have a medium sized company you'll hire people to fill those positions. If you've already performed some or all of these tasks you'll know how to describe each position to a prospective employee and it'll be easier to find the right person to work with you.

But what if you are a solo entrepreneur? You'll probably try to do everything yourself at the beginning, either because you won't have the budget to hire a staff or because you want to control every aspect of the business. Many entrepreneurs conclude that because the business is their own and they created the enterprise, it can't run without them doing everything. I've been there! I know that exact feeling. But even if you're a control freak (like me) you still need assistance.

You'll probably have to handle all these tasks yourself at first, but successful people realize they can't excel in everything. And you know what? You don't have to! But, by performing these duties yourself, at least in the beginning, you'll know how to perform them and you gain an understanding of the kind of skills required to perform each function.

Even if you can perform all the tasks required to run and grow your business, you'll limit your success if you spend every minute of your time handling tasks that are outside your core expertise and strengths. If nothing else, when you delegate tasks to people who are more qualified to handle them you can better leverage yourself and concentrate on the key tasks needed to grow your business.

It is essential to your growth and success to create what I call a "virtual team." Gather the best experts you can find in the areas you need to complete your skills and functions. These "partners" can help you think through and analyze different problems, issues, and challenges. Plus, they add a new perspective or slant to your point of view. They can offer experiences and insights you don't have. Since this small group of trusted advisors serves as consultants to you rather than employees, they are in effect "virtual." They can help you when you need their skills, expertise, and input but you don't have to worry about making a weekly payroll.

Over the last two years, I tried many different things. I joined different groups: focus groups, "Mastermind Groups," expert panels, peer groups, and a host of other groups and associations. Some groups met once a week, some once a month. We discussed our issues in business and the purpose was to brainstorm and help each other.

But with many of the groups, I noticed the people in the group changed too often. This made it more difficult to develop close relationships and discover which members could help me and which I could help. The group also lacked a solid foundation and a consistent path of development and growth. And with the changing composition of the groups, it was always challenging to get to know people in a meaningful way and even more difficult to build trust. These limitations made the members reluctant to share their personal issues and challenges.

As a result, I created my own virtual team with people I knew very well. I created a set of goals for my team and a written description of the types of people and experts and the scope of knowledge I needed.

Since I already knew many of these people and I had been in

business for a period of time, I knew what I needed had a sense of the value my team members could provide even though we wouldn't meet on a regular basis. My virtual team evolved even though we didn't create a formal agreement; we just began meeting with the general goal of helping each other. We knew we could contact each other at any time. The rule was that each person would offer their candid opinions, provide advice on an issue, or feedback on an idea to start a new program or project.

My virtual team includes: a business coach, a financial advisor, a CPA, a lawyer, a graphic designer, and a marketing consultant. And I have a friend who operates a business similar to mine. We call each other once a month to discuss our monthly goals, help each other focus on those goals, continue making progress, and stay on track. My friend isn't in the United States or France; she is in Denmark! The people on your team don't need to be right next to you or event in the same town, state, or country. They just need to be available for you and you for them when needed.

The most important goal is to find a group of people you feel confident in and comfortable with, like to work with, and trust their judgment. During the first year I was in business, I tried to accomplish everything on my own; finally I realized to be most productive and effective, I had to enlist others to help. My virtual team helps me accomplish a lot more of my goals and be more efficient and productive. Collectively, they take a lot of the pressure off my shoulders and help me become even more successful.

Who is on your team?

Build your team one person at a time; you can join a group or start your own. Consider the "Focus Group" like in my mastermind. Since they already met once or twice a month for the regular meeting, they got the chance to know each other and learn about their respective businesses. Over time they came to the point where they were able to exchange ideas more freely and openly describe and discuss more of their challenges. As a team they shared their experiences and began helping each other in a significant way. And the fact that the same group of people meets every month makes it is easier to work together over the long run and helps each other to stay focused.

PART III
Strategies to
Grow Your Visibility

CHAPTER 11
How to Make Sure Your Business Card Gets Noticed

Having organized and attended networking events for years, I'm still always surprised and amazed to see how many small business owners don't have business cards or don't have professional business cards. Having a professional business card helps portray your business image and make you stand out from the crowd. When you meet somebody you have less than 10 seconds to make the right first impression and your business card can help make sure people will remember you.

Your business card is your first marketing tool. Are you using it in the most effective way?

Many small business owners spend hours and hours trying to find the best way of marketing their businesses. But when it comes to their business cards they don't follow the same rules. Most people just include their basic contact information and don't realize how this little piece of paper can say a lot about their businesses.

When you place an ad in a newspaper or magazine, don't you try to write the most effective text to attract clients so people buy your products or services? So why not pay the same attention when designing your business card.

Your business card is your first marketing tool. Every time you give it to somebody is a chance to communicate something about your business. Your business card is often the tool which will help people decide whether they want to work with you; it's an extension of your business. When you meet somebody for the first time they'll judge you on your appearance, your clothes, the way you act, the way you speak, AND YOUR BUSINESS CARD If the whole package looks professional they'll be willing to continue the conversation with you. If it doesn't look professional they won't waste their time and will find somebody else to work with.

We used to say we shouldn't judge a book by its cover, but unfortunately people do. So put all the chances on your side.

Here are the 10 indispensable keys which need to appear on your business card:

On the front of your card:

1. Your name – this may sound obvious, but make sure it's easy to find. People need to see your name as soon as they receive your card so they'll be able to associate your face with the name on the card. This will help them to remember you.

2. Your title – if you work for a corporation, your title is always mentioned on the card. If you're a small business owner, it's important to mention if you're the founder, the CEO, the president, etc. Again, make it easy for people to remember you and what you do.

3. The name of your company – even if you're a one person operation, it's important to have a business name. Only using your name and not your company name gives the image of a part-time activity and not a serious business. It's the same as when you introduce yourself and say, "I'm a consultant" vs "I own a consulting company." Even if your consulting company is only you, this will have more impact. People won't pursue you in the same way if they can't take you seriously.

4. Your email address –don't use an email with yahoo, AOL, Gmail, or Hotmail, account. Have a professional email with yourname@yourdomainname.com. It doesn't cost a lot to buy a domain name so please invest the $10 to $15 to buy a domain and use it on your business card.

You can have a free email address you use to subscribe to

newsletters or for your personal correspondence, but is shows a lack of professionalism on your business card. Plus it's much easier for people to remember your name and your company name than a strange email with your nickname!

5. Your phone number – use the best number for people to reach you. Personally I think too many phone numbers are confusing and take up too much space. I recommend you use your main number, even if it is your cell phone, because it's the most convenient way to reach you.

6. Your website – having a website will help people to learn more about your business. Your business card can't say everything, so give them the opportunity to get the information they're looking for. Use your business card to bring traffic to your website.

7. Your logo – it's as important to have a logo as it is to have a business name. Again, it gives you a professional image. Using a white card with no logo, and just your name, phone number and email won't help people remember you. Some people use clipart on their business card and think it looks like a logo. In people's minds this is definitely not the same thing! If you aren't ready to invest in yourself how do you expect people to invest in you?

8. Your tagline – a tagline ensures people associate your company name with your product or service. A tagline is a short sentence describing your business mission and what makes you unique. It's is usually the only thing people remember after you've met. It's important to choose your words carefully when creating your tagline so you hook your audience and are memorable.

Just because you're a small business owner doesn't mean you can't use the same strategies as the big companies. Make sure you use all the marketing tools available to promote your business. This is called 'branding'. Using an effective logo & tagline are one of the most effective ways to successfully brand your business.

Take a look at most of the business cards you've collected and you'll notice few of them have taglines. Stand out from the crowd and make sure to have the key elements on your card and that they are memorable.

On the back of your card:

When I work with a client and help him or her redesign their business card, I always encourage them to use the back of the card. Remember what I said earlier, "When you place an ad in a newspaper or magazine, don't you try to write the most effective text to attract clients so people buy your products or services?"

Why are you wasting the precious space on the back of your card?

Remember your business card is a marketing tool. Use it to attract potential clients and not just to provide your contact information. Use it to pass on your business message. Few people use the back of their cards so here's an opportunity for you to be different.

9. Describe the benefits of your product or service or the benefits of working with you. Use bullet points to emphasize the purpose of your products and services. Show how you can solve their problem. Encourage people to ask you questions about your business so they want to learn more and visit your website later.

10. Tell people what to do next --. don't assume people will contact you for more information: tell them what to do. Do you want them to go to your website, sign-up for your newsletter, call you, buy your product? Tell them clearly. Offer an incentive to make sure they'll take action.

Let's say you are a coach or a financial advisor; no doubt, you have a lot of competition. What makes you unique and special? When people see your card, they will probably say, "Oh, another one!" But if you mentioned your specialties on your card it makes an immediate difference.

Take my business card as an example. When I hand it to someone, even before they read it, they say "Nice card!" First, because of the quality of the paper, thick, glossy, you can see that I didn't print the card myself. It's colorful and matches my website. The card mentions "Seminars, Workshops & Networking" which explains exactly what I do and my tagline "Build Your Business While You Build Friendships" which is the purpose of the networking meetings that I organize to help people build relationships to grow their business through networking.

What's on your Business Card?

Take a look at your card now:
- Does it include the key elements to give a professional image to your business?
- Does your card stand out from the crowd?
- Does your card give you the results you are expecting?
- Does your card say what you want it to say?
- Does your card's design work with your company image and the rest of your marketing materials?

If you have one design for your business card, a second design for your website and a third for your brochure, how do you expect people to take you seriously? Your business card is an extension of your company just like your logo, letter head, brochures, flyers, website, and any marketing tools. They must all have the same message and design.

Order professional business cards. Avoid cards you print yourself. It doesn't cost a lot to print professional business cards; you can order a thousand for $40 to $60 online and it doesn't cost much more to print on both sides of your card. But it makes an incredible difference and has a greater impact on people.

Use the same logo and colors as your website, brochure, or flyer. Having consistency on your marketing materials will help people to recognize you wherever they see you. The more they see you or your logo, the more they'll remember you and the more they'll keep in touch with you. Try to always be at the forefront of their minds.

And never leave home without your business cards! Wherever you go, to a networking event, to the dentist, to the movies, to a party, always bring your business cards with you. You never know where you'll meet an interesting new contact and you don't want to miss the opportunity to exchange cards. Writing your telephone number or email address on a piece of paper or napkin doesn't look very professional.

CHAPTER 12
How to Brand Yourself & Your Business in 30 Seconds

Did you ever meet a person at a networking event and had to think before you answered "What do you do?"

Did you ever notice how some people stumble when they are asked the defining question? Or some people just go on and on and after 5 minutes of non-stop explanation, you still don't really understand the purpose of their business? I guess at some point you were in one of these positions, if not both! How can you introduce yourself and your business in just 30 seconds, making sure you deliver both your brand and benefits of your services?

Here are the top 3 key elements to brand yourself in 30 Seconds

1. Perfect your Elevator Pitch

You want to be ready at any time so you need to prepare your answer in advance and rehearse it. The next time somebody asks you "What do you do?" you shouldn't have to think of an answer.

Start your elevator pitch by mentioning very clearly who is your target market and what their needs are: their problem. In just one or two sentences explain the benefit of your services and how you bring the solution to this target market.

Please don't say "Oh my service is for everybody!" because it isn't. If you don't have a target market with a common problem you can solve, you can't grow your business. And remember, you won't be able to grow your business if you don't know who your target market is. Take a few seconds to explain what makes you different from your competitors. What is you unique selling position? Don't try to be technical or use jargon from your industry because this generally causes people's attention to wander. Use the formula KISS (Keep It Short and Simple).

Be cautious not to tell your whole story. Instead, hook your audience; intrigue them so they'll ask you questions about you and your business. Think as if you were introducing yourself on Twitter, but instead of 140 characters, you have a few sentences to work with.

Always finish your elevator pitch with a call to action. Tell people what to do next: go to your website, sign-up for your newsletter for free report, call you for a free consultation, etc…

Practice, practice, practice – Test your elevator pitch on friends or colleagues and get their feedback. Rehearse it until you sound natural and not like reading. Say it in front of the mirror. Practice and perfect your elevator pitch to get more contacts and clients!

2. Make your Business Card Stand Out

The second step after you deliver your elevator pitch to somebody at a networking event, or after any contact, is to give your business card. If you have an effective elevator pitch but then give a crappy business card, you just lost a new potential contact. You need to have a professional image. Remember to use the back of the card to highlight the benefits of using your product or services.

3. Have a Professional Website

Obviously you don't have time to say everything you want to in 30 seconds. Your business card can't say everything either. A professional website is your greatest tool to spread effective information about you, your business, your products or services, and the benefits of working with you.

To focus on your branding, again use the same color on all of your marketing tools, business card, flyers, post cards, website etc. Having a streamlined look will ensure that people will recognize you as soon as they see your materials. If you use different colors or logos on each material, people can feel lost and as a result they will never contact you.

Now that you attracted them to your website, make sure they don't leave without taking action. You can have a nice and flashy website, but without a direct purpose and a call to action, the extra money you spend on website is wasted. You'll need an opt-in box on each and every page of your website; you never know on which page they'll decide to sign-up. You will also need an incentive for them to sign-up. Offering a bit of valuable information for free right away is the best option. Just mentioning "sign-up for my newsletter" won't do the trick.

The other advantage of having an opt-in box is you know you are contacting your target market. Who else would sign up for your newsletter? If people are not interested in your services, they won't give you their information. It's as simple as that.

Those 3 key elements will help you to build the perfect branding while reaching your target market and building your list. They work as a package, so make sure to not miss one of these important steps to grow your business.

CHAPTER 13
Stop Pitching Everybody & Start Selling to Your Target Market

I recently hosted an event and noticed, once again, one of the reasons people don't attract the right target at networking events is because they're so vague in describing their business or services that nobody can remember them. As always, I welcome everybody who attends my event, and if they are there for the first time, ask them what they do, how I can help them and, more importantly, how I can connect them with the right contact.

Here are two specific examples of "NO-NO" in networking:

First example – One attendee was recently laid off, and therefore looking for a new job. I guess this person wanted to use this opportunity to explore new areas of business, but when I asked her: "What kind of job are you looking for?" Her answer was: "Oh, I can do everything. I speak four languages, and I am ready to try anything. Do you know who I could talk to?"

I asked her to be more specific because when she says "everything", I don't know what kind of job that is. I tried to get her specialty or area of expertise but always got the same answer: "No, I don't really know what to do, I can just do everything."

How can anyone help this person, or refer her to any of their contacts? If she doesn't know what she is looking for, how can they know?

Second example – I spoke with a person from an insurance company. When I asked: "Who is your target market?" her answer was: "Everyone." Once again I tried to get a more specific answer, but she said, "I can work with everybody: individuals, professionals, corporations. Anyone who needs insurance."

So how do I help her? I can't think of each of the 3,000 people in my network; if I had a specific target, that would've helped me. For example, I know a financial advisor who specializes in people in entertainment. Since he has a niche, each time I meet somebody in this area, I think about him and can refer his name.

I also get this answer, very often from women selling cosmetics: "I can sell to everyone who has skin and hair." This isn't a specific answer! So even if we (women) all need daily cream, anti-aging cream or make up, we won't become clients just like that because they sell XYZ brand.

Did you notice that when you say to people your target market is "everybody" you usually leave without any referrals?

For me "everybody" means "nobody." That tells me a lot about the person in front of me because people who try to sell to everybody are usually the same people who struggle in their business. You just can't sell to everybody!

When you know your niche or target market, it becomes easier to communicate with your prospects and clients. Now you know how to approach them, you know their main problems, and how to solve them. You know where to find them and can network in targeted organizations. You know where to advertise because you know what they read and what their interests are. You know who they are and where to find them.

This doesn't mean that if somebody outside your target market contacts you, you will answer: "No, sorry. You're not part of my target marker, I can't work with you." When you concentrate on your target market, you attract a lot of more clients in less time.

Instead of going to every event in the city, expecting one person might be the right fit for you, join events related to your industry and your target market. Fish where the fish are.

If you want people to remember you and give you referrals, be clear and specific about what you do. Make it easy for people to help you. In other words, help them to help you. Be clear on what you do and what you want so others will be clear on what you need. Then watch the numbers of referrals you get.

CHAPTER 14
How Networking
Will Help You
Grow Your Business

No matter if you like networking or not, if you are an introvert or an extrovert, everyone needs to network: entrepreneurs, small business owners, customers, vendors, employees, employers, job seekers and so on. Networking is the key to grow your business. You can offer the best products and services in the world, but if nobody knows about you and your offering, there's no purpose.

But does everyone know how to network and make their contacts and connections count?

Many people think the purpose of networking is to sell. They attend a lot of networking events and spend lots of time meeting people for coffee. They don't even ask what the other person does but immediately give them their business card and their sales pitch. They spend a lot of energy and are surprised they don't get the results they expected.

The purpose of networking is to build relationships, ask your new contacts questions, learn more about them and their businesses to see how you can help them, what contacts, leads or referrals you can exchange.

Networking is a reciprocal game; I believe that the old adage "the more you give, the more you receive." The purpose is to get exposure, build your network of contacts, build relationships and take steps to grow your business over the long term.

1 What Networking is Not

Networking is not a numbers game.

Many people approach networking as a haphazard or random effort. Some people might approach 100 and hope to meet three people who could be helpful to them. Tut there's no certainty you will meet those "three" key people, especially at one particular event.

Focus on quality and not on quantity. Some people think they had a successful event when they collect 30 or 40 or more business cards but they are missing the real point. How many of these 30 or 40 people will you be able to follow-up with? How many of these 30 or 40 will follow-up with you? What's the value of collecting huge numbers of business cards that will end up in a shoebox? How many of these people will you have meaningful interactions with?

Networking is not a place to sell.

You have to be prepared to give your elevator pitch to introduce yourself, not give a sales pitch. If you attend an event expecting to find a new client and close a sale right away, chances are you'll be disappointed. Furthermore, the other attendees might not appreciate your attitude. If you find a new client after an event, which does happen sometimes, it's because you sent the right message and you appeared as a problem solver, not as a salesperson.

2. What Networking Is

Networking is more than just shaking hands, meeting and greeting, and collecting business cards.

- It is about building relationships and being committed to help other business professionals grow and achieve their own goals and objectives.

- It is about the quality of your contacts and not the quantity of your contacts.
- It is about consistency. The best plan is to belong to two or three groups, attend their events regularly, and get to know the other members. They'll get to know you and trust you too. When you see the same people over and over again, you'll develop stronger relationships with them. Building relationships with a committed group of people will result in new leads for your business. Instead of running to every event you can find, meeting more and more people each time and never seeing them again, a focused networking effort is likely to yield strong results.
- It is about patience. The benefits will not appear overnight. This is why you need to follow up with your contacts over time. The people and the timing must be right to develop useful business relationships. Networking is like dating: one meeting is not enough time to get to know someone. It will probably take some time, a few meetings, some lunches or drinks before you really start doing business together. And realistically you won't conduct business with all the people you meet, but they may refer people to you and vice versa. And that also creates value.

I met certain people a number of times because we were either members of the same group or ran in to each other at different events, and it took us a year or two before we even considered doing business together. But each time we met, we had the opportunity to say a little more about ourselves, to talk about our vacations, our families, and other topics that weren't related to business at all. Through those meetings, we became closer and closer. So when the time came I needed their services or they needed mine, it was obvious to work together.

CHAPTER 15
How to Maximize Your Networking Effort

1. The #1 success of networking is to show up.

When you join a group or an organization it's important you commit to the group and attend the meetings on a regular basis.

In order to build relationships with other members, they need to meet you more than once and you need to meet them more than once. The more times you attend the meetings, the more you'll get results. At each meeting, you'll learn a little more about them and their business and they'll learn more about you. The more they see you, the more they know about you, the more they trust you, the more referrals they'll give you.

2. Always arrive prepared.

Conduct some research before you decide to attend an event; you'll want to know ahead of time what kind of people will be attending. Are they in your target market, will you face a lot of competitors, or do you have a clear way to stand out from the crowd?

Spend some time on the website of the event's organizing group learn about them. Do they specialize in a specific industry? Does the group focus on small and intimate events or do they pack the room with hundreds of people?

Sometimes I have people who come to my events and are surprised to see only 12 to 15 people. It's right there on my website that the small setting is what makes Biba4Network and our meetings different from other groups' meetings. On our home page we mention: "Because networking is more than just shaking hands and collecting business cards, most of our events are limited to 15 people, to drive better results. There's more time to introduce yourself and your business to the group, more time to get to know each other, so more time to get business." If they had looked at the website first, they would have known our style and wouldn't have been surprised or disappointed.

When you go to an event, it is also important to have one or two goals in mind. Are you looking for leads, partners, new clients, services? You won't approach people the same way depending on your goal. You want to be sure to send the right message and use your time wisely.

3. Never leave home without your business cards.

I've said it before: it doesn't matter where you're going, ALWAYS have your cards with you! You never know where you'll meet an interesting new contact and you don't want to miss the opportunity to exchange cards.

Carry a pen to take notes on the back of the cards you receive; something you want to remember about the person, something they said, and something you promised to send them.

4. Have an effective elevator pitch.

We talked about this earlier in the book and this is one of the keys to successful networking. Remember to introduce yourself, and tell them the old adage "What's in it for me" or more accurately, "what's in it for them." People want to learn about you: what you're about, what you can do before they make a purchase or consider referring you to one of their valuable contacts.

When you tell others about your business, be passionate, energized and energetic. Personalize your story so that your new contacts can picture themselves as part of your story. This will help them become a part of your mission.

Then once they know you and trust you, they will either buy your services or if they don't need what you offer; they will (hopefully) refer someone else to you. If they trust you, this trust will appear in the message they send to others.

Don't have only one elevator pitch but 3 or 4, to be able to adapt your message depending of your audience.

5. DO NOT SELL.

I said it before, but I will repeat it again: DO NOT SELL. Networking events are not places to sell. Do not give a sales pitch. Just introduce yourself, who you are, what you do, how you can help people. You attend these meetings and gatherings to get contacts and build relationships, not to sell.

6. Meet people, make connections, ask about their business or services. Be curious, ask about them.

People love to talk about themselves so ask questions and more importantly, listen to their answers. Use those answers to see how you can help them, how you can assist them, what resources you can share with them. As I mentioned earlier, this will always come back to help you. People you meet will be able to help you, give you referrals and resources, even if is it not today, the time will come.

7. Be a problem solver.

People are more interested in you if you tell them how you can solve their problems and challenges instead of just telling them your story. Stand out from the crowd. In the long run, you'll win all the business you desire.

8. Go to people; don't wait for them to come to you.

Some people are very shy and they'll be happy if you make the first move. Remember people attend networking meetings to meet other people and expand their circle of contacts. Help them make it easier for others to meet you.

9. Go to events with a friend, colleague, or client and introduce people to each other.

You will be considered a "Pro Networker." People will think you know almost everybody and as a result other people will come to speak with you. This tactic puts you in the center of the group and brings people to you.

10. Present a professional image.

Maintain a brochure and/or website. Some people will probably want to learn more about your business later, so give them the opportunity to get the information in a format they can digest on their own timetable. Make it easy for people to get to know you.

I become frustrated when I meet someone and can't understand what they do. Sometimes the reason is because we met only for a few seconds or because I just didn't understand. Remember English is not my first language, so sometimes I can get "lost in translation."

But other times I don't understand because they weren't clear when they described their business. When I return home and want to look at their website to learn more about them, I notice that they don't have a website. If you don't have a website now, put this high on your to-do list. In the meantime, at least create a brochure.

11. Project the right image, make the right impression, and create the right impact.

What makes you unique? Every person I have ever met is different from all the other people I know. Everyone is unique in one way or another. This carries over into the business you create. When you display your individualism, your best traits, you'll stand out from the crowd. When you are proactive, you'll meet many new people, and you'll ensure they remember you.

12/.In the 24 to 48 hours after an event send a 'thank you' note or email to your new contacts.

Thank them for their time and reintroduce yourself in a few lines. They probably met many people during the event and your business card cannot say everything about you, especially if you had a meaningful conversation with the person. So, it's worthwhile to reinforce your introduction and reestablish that connection.

Give them the link to your website so they can learn more about you and your business. Tell them about your newsletter and invite them to subscribe. That will be the best way to stay in touch on a regular basis, so they will always know what you are up to. Hopefully, they'll forward your publication to others and expand your network further.

13. Follow-up, follow-up, follow-up.

Schedule follow-up meetings with people you had a good connection with or if you think you can help each other. Put an organizational and a follow-up system in place; don't become overwhelmed with all your business cards.

Develop your A, B, C lists to know how often you should contact people and reconnect with them. Follow up as soon as possible when someone gives you a referral. Your contact took the time to give you a referral, so don't spoil it; contact the referral source to thank them and then let them know how your interaction went. If the association works well, they'll be glad to be part of the success and more than happy to give you more contacts in the future. Volunteer to give them contacts in return.

14. Look at the big picture - Create partnerships.

Instead of looking for a potential client and working with people one at a time, look for other professionals with whom you can create partnerships.

Look for others to cross-promote your business: entrepreneurs who have businesses that complement yours, but who are not competitors or someone who has the same or similar target market as you. If you cross-promote each other, instead of having access to one potential prospect at a time, you'll have access to their entire mailing list, 100's or 1,000's of people, who are your exact target market.

Organize events together: seminars, workshops, teleclasses. You'll get more exposure in less time.

15/ Do it again and again.

You'll see how networking will expand your contacts and will help you grow your business.

CHAPTER 16
7 Easy & Powerful Ways to Become an Expert

Are you like most of those small business owners who are good at what they do but still struggle to get new clients? Do you know how or where to start promoting yourself and their businesses?

I work with a lot of new entrepreneurs and small business owners and one of the most frequent comments I hear is, "I don't have enough clients and I don't have money to spend on advertising my services. What are my options?"

There are many things you can do to promote your products or services to attract new clients. The good news is most of these marketing tools are free or cost very little. In addition to promoting your products or services, you get a chance to promote yourself and become recognized as an expert in your field.

Here are 7 Easy & Powerful Ways to Promote Your Business While You Become Recognized as an Expert:

1. Publish you own newsletter

You already know by now that after networking, publishing a newsletter is my favorite marketing tool. Your newsletter is the best way for your readers to get to know you and trust you. While your build your database your newsletter turns your leads into prospects and your prospects into clients.

2. Write articles

Regularly write articles about your field and publish them on your website, your newsletter and submit them to ezine directories and magazines. This will build your credibility and image as an expert. Being published in ezine directories will bring traffic to your website. More traffic means more people will subscribe to your newsletter and receive other information and tips from you. More people on your list means more people will buy from you!

3. Write a book or an ebook

If you are comfortable with writing you can write your own book. But if you don't want to spend months writing a book, or think you don't have enough to say, start with writing articles, then make a compilation of them and turn them into an ebook.

Creating an ebook is totally free, you just have to convert your word document into a PDF document. It takes only a few seconds. (You can download free PDF software online.)

Become a problem solver to your prospects and clients. They'll thank you for your help and buy your ebook to find the solution.

Offering a free ebook can be a great way of attracting more people to sign-up to your newsletter. When you sign-up for my Newsletter at www.TheConnectionqueen.com you receive my free ebook "15 Ways to Instantly Skyrocket Your Networking Results".

4. Host your own teleclass

Hosting your own teleclass is the same concept as writing an article but in this case you help people over the phone instead of on paper. It's better because you get a chance to speak to your audience directly, answer their questions, and solve their problems. You also get instant exposure. Plus, hosting a teleclass is free. You can use various bridge lines, most are free and very easy to use. If you are not totally confident in becoming a speaker and hosting your teleclass, you can interview an expert. He or she will do most of the talking but you'll still take credit since you're the one bringing the resources to your audience.

5. Create a product

With your teleclass, it is even easier to create a product instantly. While you host your teleclass, the only thing you'll have to do is to record it. As soon as you finish the teleclass, you can either sell the recording on your website or offer it for free as a sample of your program.

The same applies when creating a video. You can either record yourself doing a presentation or a live event and sell it on your website, or offer it for free as a sample of your program.

6. Start public speaking

Spread the word by offering your expertise at live events, associations, networking events, and conferences. Select organizations whose members are your target market so you become THE expert in your field and build-up your name, your credibility, and your newsletter list.

7. Say again & again you're an expert and people will follow you.

Come up with a name for yourself, so people can easily remember you. Muhammad Ali called himself "The Greatest" long before he became a champion but years later everybody knew his nickname.

The first time somebody called me "The Connection Queen" years ago, I found it weird but quickly realized the impact it had on people. I started using it more and more, until I became confident enough to actually use it as my new brand and create my website www.TheConnectionQueen.com

Become "THE GO TO GUY" in your field and you will quickly realize that people will come to you for your expertise.

PART IV
Next Steps & Moving Forward

CHAPTER 17
Take Action Now!

Congratulations, you made it to the end of the book! So I hope you are more motivated than ever to start your own business or you got some ideas to reenergize, grow, redirect and reposition your existing business.

Just reading a book isn't going to help you Start Your Dream Business Today! Now, you need to take action to create the business and life of your dreams. There are lots of action steps for you to do. I suggest that you re-read this book and decide on one action from each chapter that you can get started with. Some of the action steps might be more fun or interesting than others but they are all important.

If you haven't started your business yet, a great place to start your project will be with the eight questions in Chapter 1 you should ask yourself before you start your business. If you've already started your business, it's not too late to do more research about your industry. You should also write or update your business plan.

Some of the steps outlined in this book can be taken out of order; it's never too late to review your business card and perfect your elevator pitch.

There are other chapters of the book you'll want to re-read regularly. There are action steps you may do many times over the course of your business, like identifying your ideal client. Sometimes your ideal client will change as your business changes and grows. Use this book as a guide to growing your business and creating a life you love.

Especially pay attention to Chapter 10 "Why You Need A Team of Experts. Nobody can build a business on their own; everyone needs help, expert advice, and to learn from someone who has done it before. This is especially true when you're working on an aspect of your business you might not have focused on enough in the past.

The time to Start Your Dream Business is NOW!

You would need to be completely committed in this new venture, from starting your business, making it successful, and improving your existing business. Be ready to probably spend night and day in the beginning to make it happen. But the reward is worth it.

Forget about all the reasons why you can't and focus on what you have: your drive to succeed, the tools outlined in this book, and your desire to live the life of your dreams.

If you are driven to become a successful entrepreneur, nothing will stop you. As Zig Ziglar wrote "See you at the top". Reading this book is a great first step!

To help you to turn your passion into profit and have the success you deserve, here is my free gift for you as a bonus. To get a lot more tips and advices from me and other famous and successful entrepreneurs, go to www.BibaPedron.com/bonus-book

Work With Biba

Since I started my first business in 1998, I have grown two international businesses specializing in helping people like you develop their business with effective networking, social media and marketing strategies. I have shared my strategies with hundreds of people and guided them to tweaking those strategies to their own businesses. When you discover my systems, you will be excited and amazed at how easily you connect with your target market, expand your business and double your revenue.

I am also recognized in France as one of the top female business coach and marketing expert.

My goal is to help and advise you on all aspect of your own business to show you the strategies that I use over and over again for myself in my successful 6-figure international businesses and that I teach to my clients. This is your chance to learn how to boost your income, network effectively, attract more clients and get your brand known.

To learn more about how you can work with me to grow your business, please visit me at www.TheConnectionQueenBlog.com

About The Author

Biba Pédron was born and raised in France. For over 15 years, she has served as a sales & marketing manager for a number of companies in her native France. Recognized as someone who powerfully connects with people, professionally and socially, Biba brings her successful networking techniques to both sides of the Atlantic.

With great passion and drive, and little English language speaking skills, she moved to the U.S. in 2003 and within two years became known as "The Connection Queen" and published her first book, Start Your Dream Business Today.

Business coach & marketing expert, Biba helps countless small business owners, entrepreneurs and professionals connect the dots of marketing, social media, networking, and branding to grow their business, teaching simple but effective marketing strategies that really work. So they can attract more clients online and offline while building a 6-figure business. All while following their passion and doing what they love best.

Biba Pédron knows from experience that the majority of businesses don't succeed because they lack the right tools and the right system needed to excel. This is why she offers entrepreneurs, key business secrets needed to build their business and give them the exact formula they need to grow their business in a step-by-step road map, leaving them with no way to get lost or take a wrong turn.

Over the past 10 years she not only taught networking and marketing strategies to her clients, she also connected thousands of entrepreneurs to build international partnerships.

Biba is the author of "Start Your Dream Business Today", "Power of Networking Secrets", "15 Ways to Instantly Skyrocket Your Networking Results", "Top 10 Closet Must-Haves to Successful Business Style", and various books in French.

To learn more about Biba, please visit www.BibaPedron.com